C000142189

In memory of Douglas who loved Whitebrook

D.M.B.

For Meg

E.H.B.R.

For the people of Whitebrook, past and present,
for making this publication possible.

D.M.B. & E.H.B.R.

Edited by

DIANA BEVAN was born in Cheltenham in 1932, studied English Language and Literature at Bristol, followed by a Diploma in Social Studies at Birmingham. In between moving round the country with her mining engineer husband and raising their 3 sons she worked as a psychiatric social worker and a guardian ad litem, completing her education with an M.Phil in Social Work at York. She and her late husband moved to Whitebrook in 1990.

ELEANOR REES was born in 1975 and brought up in Shropshire. She graduated from the University of Wales Aberystwyth with a BA (Hons) in American Studies and a Masters Degree in Historical Studies. Living in Whitebrook, she works part-time as an archivist whilst caring for her three year old daughter.

An iron pipe for carrying water from Manor Brook to drive the wheel at Clearwater Mill, circa 1990s. Photographer: Mike Sturt.

This book has been produced by Whitebrook Conservation Group as a direct result of the *Whitebrook – Then & Now* Exhibition of March 2004. Many of the hundreds of visitors, who attended the exhibition held in the village of Whitebrook in the Wye Valley felt that permanent records should be made available to a wider audience.

Its production has relied almost entirely on the generous contributions, in the form of recollections and photographs, from residents of the community, past and present. Whilst readers will be able to have a taste of Whitebrook's industrial past, it is hoped that the community, then and now, is brought to life through some amusing and poignant tales along with some fascinating and striking photography.

Bell Outing organised by the landlord, Mr Probert, circa 1950s.

WHITEBROOK in the 21st century is truly an area of outstanding natural beauty with its trees and its abundance of flora and fauna. It is also an area of tranquillity, its peace being disturbed only by the occasional car or aeroplane, wild bird song, the crowing of a cockerel, the barking of dogs and, of course, the sound of the brook.

The Whitebrook might even have inspired Tennyson, were it not for the fact that in the 19th century and earlier, other sounds would have been heard along its banks – the sounds of the mills.

Kiln Tump Quarry (situated between Whitebrook and Penallt, next to the common land), 1908.

On 6th June, 1607, in order to meet the increasing demand for brass wire, the Governors Assistants and Socyetie of the Cyttie of London for the Mineral and Battery Works obtained a 99 year lease on

"…a tract of land along the Whitebrooke to the Wye…to erect mills for the drawing or making of wire…"

An indenture on the same date refers to the fact that

"…by and through the (?) hillside of wch said grounde called the Manney last mentioned is also a new dich (a leat) lately digged by the said Governors Assistants and Socyetie or their assignes extending in length from the said Manney Brook to certen newe workehouses now also lately erected upon the said Manney side and intended to be used for drawing of iron wyer by water and water wheels and alsoe divers other cottages and smale dwelling howses and foundacions for houses are in like manner erected…"

Following a decline in the industry the wireworks ceased to operate in about 1720. Very little documentary evidence has been found but it is considered that

there were two, and possibly up to six wireworks (Coates, 1992). The location of the sites is unclear. They were all water powered, however, and the various water courses, ponds and leats may indicate their locations. The passage of time, and the probability that the mills were taken over for other purposes for example paper mills, (it is probable that the paper mills at Traligael, Clearwater & the Wye Valley Mills originated as wireworks) means that very little identifiable evidence remains. Two other possible sites put forward by Professor D. G. Tucker are :-

● on the footpath from Holy Trinity church to the Narth

● on high ground above Tump Farm and there is evidence of the remains of buildings at both sites (Cross, undated). Some forty years after the demise of the wireworks the first paper mills appeared in Whitebrook. Apart from providing a plentiful supply of pure water, the Whitebrook also powered the engines which were used to pulverise the rags. Rags were brought in by boat to Chepstow and transported overland. Later, the mills imported esparto grass from Spain for use in the manufacturing process.

Mr Wilfrid Pick, previously of Whitebrook, recalled that local children were given 1d [one penny] a bag for old rags collected and brought to the mills. He could remember seeing some machinery in two of the mills during his childhood (Harris, 1968).

" My husband's grandfather, Mr W. Pick of the Pool Farm…had a barge…The barge brought back [from Chepstow] the grasses which were used at Whitebrook Paper Mills to make the old white £5 notes. I think it also used to take the finished paper down the river as well."
RECOLLECTIONS OF MRS W. PICK, WATERY LANE, MONMOUTH.

There were two warehouses and a quay at the point where the Whitebrook joins the Wye. These were probably available for storage of raw materials and finished paper (Coates, 1992).

Charles Heath, writing at the turn of the 19th century, stated that the mills "at Whitebrook, do not, like some of their brethren, sell a ream of paper to any pedlar that calls for it, the whole of their manufactory being consigned to that city [Bristol] to which it finds a ready, as well as cheap water conveyance, and from where they receive their raw materials" (Harris, 1968).

Manufactured products from the Whitebrook mills included bank note, brown wrapping, cartridge and printing paper (Coates, 1992).

At the beginning of the nineteenth century all paper was made by hand and in single sheets. Later, machinery was installed, which would speed up production and improve on quality.

With an expanding market for paper the number of mills increased. By 1793 there were five / six mills and five are still identifiable.

The 19th century saw the gradual decline of papermaking in Whitebrook. There was a lack of continuity and businesses did not seem to pass from father to son. As the century progressed mills changed hands more frequently and, although attempts were made to revive them through investment in new machinery, the industry in Whitebrook had ceased by about 1880.

The building of the Wye Valley Railway in 1875 seemed to offer the industry wider access to raw materials and markets but, in this period, Whitebrook was never stable enough to warrant a railway siding. In fact the railway allowed paper making to move nearer major towns, where labour and materials did not depend on water transport and where there was an easily accessible market for paper. It would seem that the railway network helped the demise of the industry in Whitebrook.

Over 600 people worked in the Whitebrook paper mills in the 19th century though not all of them lived in the village but walked from the neighbouring communities. The censuses of 1841 and 1851 show that a sizeable proportion were not born in Monmouthshire and many had moved with their families from as far as Scotland and London. This was not a new phenomenon since the wireworks attracted immigrants from central

Europe in the early 17th century. The paper works offered a variety of jobs from managers, skilled craftsmen such as joiners and spokemakers, to the lowly rag-pickers. These unfortunates had to sort the dirty rags prior to the soaking process and were mainly elderly men and women. Their lot must have been hard enough in the 1840s when the mills were in full production but by 1851 there was a slump as foreign imports became cheaper. A widow in her seventies in the earlier census was reported as an unemployed rag-picker ten years later. Since she lived alone one wonders how she managed.

When the community was thriving there was a wide variety of trades to support it, including innkeepers, shoemakers, tailors, bonnetmakers, carriers and smiths. At the same time the traditional rural occupations continued alongside the industries.

There were farmers, agricultural labourers, farriers, foresters, millers, millwrights, masons, fishermen as well as the other trades associated with the river. Women not working in the paper mills were mainly servants, barmaids and laundresses, though one was a nurse and another lucky enough to be an annuitant.

After the decline of the paper mills and later the flour mills, people drifted away from the area to find work elsewhere, leaving behind a largely agricultural community or one where the breadwinner worked in Monmouth, Chepstow or Redbrook. The twenties and thirties brought depressed times and local people needed to rely on traditional ways of supplementing their income by growing their own vegetables, keeping pigs and chickens and maintaining the old cider orchards, relics of which can still be seen. Gradually the area became more prosperous and newcomers improved and extended the old cottages. Min y Nant is now a substantial country house but up to the 1970s was two semi-detached cottages which had been the smithy. Similarly, Wyedene House replaced a bungalow which had originally been a ferret house. Just as the houses have changed, so too have the occupations of their inhabitants, ranging from entrepreneurs, a jeweller, a novelist, playwrights, a TV documentary maker, aeronautical scientists, a computer specialist and academics whilst still retaining some of the traditional ones such as dentists, a nurse, teachers and police officers.

1 Thomas John Davies (31.08.1851) on the left, with daughter Rhoda (12.02.187 in arms, Maria Davies of Four Chimneys (12.05.1855) on the left in the front row with Florence on her lap (31.01.1877), circa 1877.

2 Five generations at Four Chimneys, the home of Maria Davies. Pictured are Mar Davies (Great Great Grandmother), Rhoda Beach (Great Grandmother), Sybil Morgan (Grandmother), Phylis Fidler (Mother) and Pat Fidler (Baby), circa 1941.

3 Clarice Holmes (daughter of Cecil and Lilian Holmes) outside her home, the cottage now named 'Brook Cottage', circa 1937.

Riverside Warehouses, pre 1961 when they were removed. Apparently, in the early 1900s, human bodies found floating in the river were stored in these warehouses before collection by undertakers.

The paper mills were not the first mills to be established in Whitebrook. The remains of two corn mills can still be seen (Tucker, 1972).

The Grist Mill on Manor Brook has been converted into a house. The mill race & wheel pit are still visible.

Grist Mill on Manor Brook, circa 1990s. Photographer: Mike Sturt.

New Mills, (Cross, undated) was in use in the 1920s but is now roofless. The shell is maintained for posterity and the wheel pit can still be seen (Coates, 1992).

Harry Robbins (age 10) standing on the wheel at New Mills, 1925, from a Roy Williams Transparency (Staple Hill, Bristol). The Robbins family lived at New Mills until the 1920s, if not longer.

Before the council sprayed the verges from the Whitebrook crossroads to the Peckett Stone, there were win berries, orchids, cowslips, ferns and many wild flowers and at home, in the angle of the stone steps on the odd summer evening, they were lit by glow worms and, in spite of the ruins about us, it was heaven.

I purchased the land from the Crown and the mill, which dated from the 17th century, had been worked by Mr Robbins, the miller. Sadly, after I purchased the mill it was looted for iron, which was in short supply after the war and even the wheel was decimated but the fine French mill stones were left. These stones were apparently better than the English as they were able to produce a finer flour.

Downstairs, in the backroom, was either a stone or slate slab where the pig was salted after slaughter. Adjacent to one of the barns was a cider press. Alas, conservation was not my priority, only survival, and we had to move things for the sake of access.

The most important person in our family was a Mr Bert Morgan, who answered my advert and said that he would give us a "try" in two weeks to see if we "suited" – it extended for many years until arthritis limited his mobility.

I am uncertain as to the source of the following information but Bert, approximately 5 ft 2 ins, a forester, was put in charge of a gang of German POWs, who patted him on the back and said they would look after him!

I also remember a mole catcher. I paid 6d or 9d for every mole caught, but after a while the animal started to look familiar!

A Mrs Whitehead who lived at Traligael, would regularly leave her car at Whitebrook Halt and go to Chepstow by train. One day she had been on the train for about ten minutes when she realised that she had left some important papers in her car. She pulled the communication cord, the train ground to a halt and the engine driver came down to see what was wrong. She explained her dilemma and asked if anyone would miss an appointment if the train was delayed. He then shunted the train back. She retrieved her papers and they went on their way!

MEMORIES OF NEW MILLS BY MRS. WHITMORE, A FORMER RESIDENT, MARCH 2004.

1 New Mills, taken from a painting by local artist Donald Floyd. Mount Pleasant can be seen in the background.

2 Bert Morgan at New Mills, circa 1970s.

Wedding party at Whitebrook Halt (Bride - Lena Bishop, née Lerwill of the Cider Press, Manor Brook), circa 1955. Joan Davies, née Adams of Fern Bank is on the right of the picture with her coat resting on her shoulders.

WHITEBROOK HALT WAS OPENED ON 1ST FEBRUARY, 1927.

Whitebrook was served by a little steam train, the line later to be closed with the Beeching Axe in 1958. A great deal of hardship was experienced because of this and a number of older people just left their homes for pastures new, leaving them a very remunerative speculation for second homes, of which there were seven within a short distance of Springwater. When grants were available for improvement, they did not actually benefit the people who were in need of them, as a percentage of the cost had to be paid, and most residents of small homes could not raise that money, but they were a cinch for the wealthier invaders. We missed the train dreadfully, as Dad's only transport to get to work was a Moped, a cycle with a motor attached. I hardly left the village for 9 years, except when I walked to Bigsweir Bridge to catch the bus to Monmouth or Chepstow, to the dentist or for clothes or hardware.

We later purchased a three wheeler Reliant. I christened it 'a biscuit tin on wheels' but at least it kept Dad dry and warmer on his trip to Chepstow and back each day. This lasted us well and we just sat on a stool or cushions. We were later able to get a REAL car; still a three wheeler, but NEW.

When Dad used the moped, and later a motorbike, he had the inclemency of the weather to cope with all the way to Chepstow, where the ferryboats were moored, then the crew had to row to the ferryboat in a small rowboat, complete with all the weather proof clothes necessary for whatever the River Severn estuary dealt out in its tempestuous moods.

MEMORIES OF LIFE AT SPRINGWATER COTTAGE, WHITEBROOK (1952 – 1977) BY **MARY LEWIS.**

Tom Lerwill, Cider Press, circa 1930s.

My parents, Jack and Cissie Lewis, plus my elder sister and I, moved to Park Farm in July 1947 when I was just six weeks old. It was a small farm of about 22 acres and we kept cattle, sheep, chickens, ducks, geese and, of course, pigs! Everyone, however small, kept at least one pig then, to eat the household scraps and later to provide delicious home cured bacon. The flitches were hung in the kitchen and sliced as required. My father grew his own corn and root crops such as mangolds, turnips and swedes. In line with common practice in those days, a row or two of potatoes would be planted alongside the roots 'for the house'.

In about 1952 mains water pipes were installed in the area by 'Norwest'. Prior to that, we relied on water 'bucketed' from our well situated about 100 yards from the house, for our daily needs and those of the livestock. In times of exceptionally dry weather the cattle had to be driven down the road to drink from the brook at New Mills.

Until the mid 1960s a horse provided the sole motive power for the farm. 'Dobbin' was then replaced by the ubiquitous 'Little Grey Fergie'. We still keep cattle and sheep, but the 'house cow', pigs and poultry have sadly gone. I do miss having a working horse on the holding…some day perhaps?

MEMORIES OF PARK FARM BY **DOREEN WARMINGTON-GARDNER**, 2004.

1 Mavis Mardle (sitting milking a cow) pictured with her mother and Phyllis Ford, circa 1940. Mavis Mardle and Phyllis Ford were evacuated to Spring Cottage, Penyfan, the home of Mr and Mrs Morgan.

2 Joan Davies, née Adams, feeding chickens in the field above her home, Fern Bank, circa 1935.

In 1943 the small top ruin of a house, that had at one time been occupied, was later converted into a cider press where my father-in-law made his cider.

The orchard had many apple and pear trees in it that could be for eating or cider making. Also there was plum and damson.

The orchard and the field nearer the house were all in the property, the nearer field being for poultry and a sty for two pigs.

In late March and April the orchards were covered with daffodils and people in cars would ask if they could pick them. Dorothy's father used to mow the hay in the orchard and sell it to a farmer.

In the late 19th century, cider was the staple drink of the agricultural population and Whitebrook folk were no exception. Most cider makers were smallholders, who supplemented their income by producing cider.

Traditionally cider was made using stone mills. These were stone structures on which a horse pulled a heavy stone runner around in a circular trough and was a fairly slow process.

There were several cider mills in Whitebrook, namely Fern Bank, New Mills Farm and Tump Farm. In addition there were small scale presses at Cider Press Cottage, Springwater, Dawn Cottage and a cider house at Lion's Oak.

EXTRACTS FROM A LETTER, CIRCA 1993, FROM **CHARLIE** AND **DOROTHY SOUTHERN** TO THE OWNERS OF DAWN COTTAGE. DOROTHY WAS BROUGHT UP AT DAWN COTTAGE BY HER FOSTER PARENTS, JOHN AND ELIZABETH BENNETT.

1 New Mills Barn during conversion, circa 1995. The lower level was a cider press in the late 19th century to early 20th century, if not before.

2 Kingfisher Cottage, pre-1914. The property was run as a cider house by the name of 'Lion's Oak' at an earlier date.

3 The Cider Press, Fern Bank, circa 2000.

Dawn Cottage, circa 1930s. Although it looks like two, it was one cottage at this point.

Springwater was originally a cider press surrounded by orchards and is situated on the very steep, narrow lane that runs between Whitebrook and Pen-y-Fan. Most of the fruit trees have now disappeared but we still have two very large Perry pear trees that still fruit, an old gnarled cherry plus a couple of sad old apple trees.

On the day we decided to buy Springwater – a glorious August afternoon – the only sounds to be heard were the Manor Brook spilling below and a pair of buzzards mewing above. The day we moved in – a bleak horrendous Thursday in November – we had torrential rain and gales. We found that the transit van we had hired to ferry our belongings from the pantechnicon, parked in the village, would only come up the hill to Springwater when it was EMPTY so every load came up in the transit and towed behind our old four wheel drive Subaru. What a car, what a day!

Our life in Whitebrook started with difficulty. What we thought would be a £20 electrical job turned out to be more than £600 and took more than half our savings. We were skint and, to this day, are grateful for the kindness of Mike and Tiggy Sturt who lived at The Bell. They gave us cords of wood and the Rector Reverend Julian White, who obtained coke from his previous parish of Llanwern. We survived and the sun came out.

WRITTEN FOR THE WHITEBROOK *THEN & NOW* EXHIBITION, MARCH 2004, BY THE LEWIS FAMILY WHO BOUGHT SPRINGWATER COTTAGE IN NOVEMBER 1989.

Tump Farm, that was Enos Morgan's. The Morgans were perfect screams…Terrible people for cider…and on Sunday mornings when you did go down there, there was always a gathering of all the locals sitting on blocks of wood in the cellar there, tree stumps they were. They used to sit around on these blocks on a Sunday morning with the cider, a hogshead of it, in the middle or thereabouts…they always had a saucepan of cider on the hob.. and as soon as you went in there you had a glass of hot cider with two spoonfuls of sugar in it…he used six pounds of sugar from Friday until Tuesday with cider alone.

RECOLLECTIONS OF **NURSE SCUSE,** DECEASED, DISTRICT NURSE AT TRELLECH AND LLANDOGO, CIRCA 1950s.

Tump Farm, circa 1990s.
Photographer: Mrs Diana Bevan.

Joan Davies is the only person currently living in the valley who was born here before 1962. Her parents, Maggie and George Adams, lived at Fern Bank with her maternal grandfather, Charles Morris, who was a forestry worker. In later life he worked on the nets on the River Wye and then at Bigsweir Estate.

In the 1930s Joan's parents opened the Youth Hostel, the building between their house and the village hall, which had previously served as a cider press. It was open from Easter until October and attracted about 1200 cyclists and walkers each year. Motorists were not allowed to stay there. When the Second World War began, the hostel and its equipment was requisitioned for the evacuees who came to Whitebrook from Birmingham, London and Folkestone.

Joan attended the village school which was in the little room attached to the church.
She can remember a time when there were very few trees on the slopes in Whitebrook. She also saw the demise of the railway, the shop, the petrol pump, the school and the chapel.

JOAN DAVIES' RECOLLECTIONS, FERN BANK 2004.

Maggie Adams of Fern Bank (centre) with friend (left) and Charlie Byatt, the postmaster (right), outside Whitebrook Post Office (now named 'Manor Brook'), circa 1950.

Group including Folkestone evacuees, circa 1940.
Left to right – Ron Taylor (evacuated to St Briavels), Joan Adams (Whitebrook resident, Fern Bank), Reg Taylor (evacuated to St Briavels), Alma Swallow (evacuated to Fern Bank), Daphne Taylor (evacuated to Fern Bank), Betty Taylor (evacuated to Fern Bank). All of the evacuees pictured were from Folkestone. The Taylors were brothers and sisters, the boys being sent to St Briavels and the girls to Whitebrook.

Joan Adams with her parents George and Maggie Adams, taken in the garden at their home, Fern Bank, circa 1938.

I remember 'Boy' Fowler's grandfather kept The Bell, then there was Mr Brown, and then a Mr Scanlon, an Irishman...he had a lovely little wife. She hated the pub. It was only 2 1/2d. a pint, beer was then.
RECOLLECTIONS OF **MRS HARRIS**, THE NARTH. MRS HARRIS LIVED IN THE BUNGALOW OPPOSITE FERNSIDE [MILL HOUSE]. HER SISTER WAS A MAID FOR THE BROWNS AT FERNSIDE IN THE 1920s.

Mrs Probert at The Bell was a very quiet little person...Well, she was as quiet as he was the other way about, because Herbie always had plenty to say, and always something comical.
RECOLLECTIONS OF **NURSE SCUSE**, DECEASED, DISTRICT NURSE AT TRELLECH & LLANDOGO.

Herbie Probert was at The Bell. He was a nice fellow, a real old sport, I liked him.

I remember saying to him years ago, "I wouldn't live down this blooming old Whitebrook for all the world, for it's so closed in", and he said to me "I wouldn't live up this old Beacon for all the world!" He was always joking about something. He was really nice. He wasn't a publican to look at. He was a little thin, not very short, just a medium man, slightly built.
RECOLLECTIONS OF **NURSE SCUSE**, DECEASED, DISTRICT NURSE AT TRELLECH & LLANDOGO.

Probert's mother used to keep The Gockett. There was an old man at Penallt who had a car and he couldn't drive it very well. Probert was delivering coal at that time...This car had beautiful brass headlamps and had a high-up seat. He got in the ditch by the cross roads and couldn't get out, and Herbie Probert

came along in his lorry and pulled him out, and [the old man] was so overwhelmed with gratitiude...that he turned round to wave at Probert and went straight back in the ditch again. "Silly old bu**er!" said Probert - and he would tell this story without laughing. Mrs Probert hated the pub business.
RECOLLECTIONS OF **MRS HARRIS**, THE NARTH. MRS HARRIS LIVED IN THE BUNGALOW OPPOSITE FERNSIDE [MILL HOUSE]. HER SISTER WAS A MAID FOR THE BROWNS AT FERNSIDE IN THE 1920s.

Mrs Holmes at The Crown used to say "You wake up in the morning and you get wood for breakfast, wood for lunch, wood for tea." She used to find those trees very oppressive.
RECOLLECTIONS OF **NURSE SCUSE**, DECEASED, DISTRICT NURSE AT TRELLECH & LLANDOGO.

1 *Bell Outing organised by the landlord, Mr Probert, circa 1950s.*

2 *Drinkers outside The Bell, circa 1950. Donald Goddard (2nd on left), Jim Evans, Crossing House (3rd on left), Mr Probert, landlord (6th on left).*

main picture
The Bell in the snow, circa 1963.

top Jane (mother), Mary Jane (daughter) and John (father)
Reynolds taken outside The Crown, pre-1907. The Reynolds
family ran the inn at this time.
© The Nelson Museum, Monmouth

bottom John Reynolds, landlord, pictured at the side of The
Crown, pre-1914. © The Nelson Museum, Monmouth

Whitebrook Billiards Team Supper, The Crown, circa 1952.

Austin Durrant (Cider Press), Reg Hussey (Min-y-Nant) & Colin Pick (Wye Mount) at Leo Williams' funeral (formerly of Sunnybank), pictured outside The Bell. The funeral was held at the Baptist Chapel. In their youth they polished coffins for an undertaking business run at The Crown by William Burley.

An annual event that I would look forward to was fireworks at Tump Farm. Watching a fantastic display whilst feasting on baked potatoes cannot be beaten. The village hall BBQ stirs up many memories also, trying to attract the older boys' attention and always giving in to dancing with rather worse-for-wear adults at the end of the night.

Another annual village event is the carol service at the Bisses in which Dad or one of the boys usually end up singing a duet in 'We Three Kings' and, considering they all have a one note limit and this note differs between them, a fairly dreadful noise ensues! I do admire them for their courage.

VICKI GAUNT, WYE VALLEY HOUSE, 2004. VICKI IS A STUDENT AT HABERDASHERS MONMOUTH SCHOOL FOR GIRLS.

Pilstone House, circa 1940s.

Pilstone House including kitchen garden, circa 1940s.

ROSIE BISS REMEMBERS:-

"A Christmas concert at the church and walking on a frosty night through the village, lit with oil lamps with my cello tied around my neck with dressing gown cord.

Sitting on Basil the donkey; I told him all my problems and he was sensitive and understanding.

Snowy, our other donkey, who in a previous life worked on the sands at Weston-Super-Mare.

My sisters and I sometimes had romantic ideas about playing our violins and cellos outside, but it never worked: no acoustic and too much competition from the birds."

ROSIE BISS, 2004.

ROSIE STUDIED MUSIC AT CAMBRIDGE UNIVERSITY AND AT MUSIC MUSIKHOCHSCHULE IN COLOGNE.

Hannah, Rosie and Clara Biss grew up in Pilstone House. All of them are now professional musicians. The Biss family's candlelit carol concerts at Pilstone House are part of what makes living in Whitebrook special.

Hannah, Rosie and Clara Biss, Pilstone House, circa late 1980s.

Patrick Grist spent 1940 to 1944 at Pilstone Farm in Whitebrook. His father brought his wife and Patrick to a safe area as their home town of Folkestone was a prime invasion target. Mr Grist found work assisting the farmer who was also a butcher. Patrick and the farmer's son became firm friends. Patrick, aged 7, and his pal, aged 5, worked on the land and Patrick actually drove the tractor!

He recalls seeing a whole column of mounted Indian troops riding through Llandogo. It took two hours for them all to pass. He also remembers that the railway line through Whitebrook was quiet during the week with only a single carriage using it, but on Sundays enormous goods trains came through, bringing war materials to Cardiff and Newport docks. Large convoys of transporters brought tanks to Bigsweir Bridge, where they were unloaded, driven across and then put back on their transporters on their way to the docks as well.

Patrick saw a poster displayed at Bigsweir station, warning people about a butterfly bomb which the Germans had started dropping by parachute. It was brightly coloured and intended to attract children and blow them to pieces. He can also recall the glow in the night sky from the fires caused by the bombing raids on Bristol and Avonmouth docks. Apparently Chepstow Racecourse was a staging post for Superfortress bombers, flying from the USA to be refitted for operational duties.

One of his other memories is of the Botteri family who lived next door at Pilstone House. Mr Botteri was Italian and was therefore interned on the Isle of Man as an enemy alien, although his wife was allowed to retain her Italian housekeeper. When they left, the house was empty for about a year and then five or six families from the East End of London were billeted there. They were fleeing from the V1 rockets or doodlebugs. According to Patrick, the children trashed both the house and garden. He believes they attended Llandogo School.

Patrick returned for the *Whitebrook Then & Now* Exhibition in 2004, having kept in touch with his host family for 60 years. His old playmate, who now lives in

1 Harold Durrant of the Cider Press (Manor Brook), circa mid 1930s. He died early in World War II as an air gunner.

2 Evacuees, many of whom would have attended Whitebrook School, circa 1940. Mavis Mardle (4th from right) and Phyllis Ford (3rd from right) were evacuated to Spring Cottage, Penyfan, the home of a lady called Mrs Morgan.

Raglan, met him in the Village Hall and, while they were reminiscing, Roger Brown from the shop in Llandogo recognised them and reminded Patrick that he was the 'little so and so' who had taken to the river on a tractor tyre and nearly been washed over the weir!

There were other evacuees present, all delighted to see Joan Davies, a long-standing Whitebrook resident, who remembered them all. Mavis Pearsall (née Bishop) had a clear recollection of arriving on the train from Birmingham with her sister and other evacuees. They walked from the Halt to the hall, where a group of residents were waiting to offer them a home. She and her sister became more despondent as child after child was picked but they were not. Eventually the

only people in the hall were the billeting officer, Mavis, her sister, a third little girl and one potential hostess. They were cast down when she said she only wanted to take one child but in the end she agreed to take all three saying they would have to sleep in the same bed. They did, but the third little girl soon went back to Birmingham. It seemed that most of the evacuees remembered their time in Whitebrook with affection.

Home Guardsmen Jack Morgan (Tump Farm) pictured on the left, alongside Mr Reynolds, circa 1940s. Mr Reynolds stayed at Tump Farm.

The local Home Guard pictured outside The Bell. Left to right are Mr Fowler (Folly Cottage), Bill Durrant (Grist Mill), Harold Lane (Kinsons Farm) and on the far right is Mr Probert (The Bell), circa 1941.

Whitebrook Farm was formerly the mill owner's house for the mill known as 'The Glyn'. This mill was in use from about 1800 until 1850 and was located a few hundred yards from the mouth of the brook. It was relatively small and was probably a hand mill, utilising water power from a dam situated behind it and a pond which is now derelict (Coates, 1992).

Whitebrook Farm, circa 1961. Photographer: Marie Hambrook, née Carstairs, former wartime evacuee at Clearwater Cottage.

I always thought it was July 3rd 1940, but some say it was June. Anyway, we children of St Eanswythes School, Folkestone had to be at St Mary's School, Folkestone, to catch a coach to Folkestone station, complete with gas mask, label on our coats and clothes in a case.

I believe the train used by us was one used by the soldiers evacuated from Dunkirk. I remember it was very warm, my mother had dressed me in a liberty bodice which I took off! We had teachers with us; Miss Wright, Miss Chidwick and Miss Wood, and some mothers; Mrs Tiltman, her sister Mrs Tompkinson and Mrs Amon. We stopped once and flasks were handed out to get some water at a colliery, but the train moved off before we could get them back. It must have been Monmouth station we arrived at and we were taken to a hall, it could have been the Rolls Hall. Some children had to have medicals, we didn't.

A lady came along, Mrs Prim Williams of Clearwater Cottage (Billeting Officer for Whitebrook), with her step-son Ron who was in the Air Force. They said, "We will have that one", and picked me. I went with them in their car, and followed the coach to Llandogo, where some children were dropped off at the hall, and then on to Whitebrook where children were allocated.

After the Battle of Britain, my mother came and joined me at the Williams'. Mr Williams had a workshop opposite Clearwater, by the chimney where he and Gilbert Morgan made pit props. We could not stay there as Lena Williams, daughter Jo and son David arrived from Bognor Regis. Lena was expecting a baby, so my mother and I moved into Glyncote Farm with the Higgins', where we had two rooms, and our furniture was moved from Folkestone.

We went to church services with Gran Fowler playing the organ. She had cats with extra toes. We also had Sunday school in the chapel with Mr and Mrs Scuse and Mrs Scuse's father Mr Hodgson. There used to be a Sunday school picnic to the 'Maypole' at Pen-y-fan. We also had concerts at Llandogo and had to walk home afterwards, seeing and hearing the air raids over Bristol.

RECOLLECTIONS OF **MARIE HAMBROOK**, NÉE CARSTAIRS, 24TH FEBRUARY 2004

Mrs Prim Williams, outside her home, Clearwater Cottage, 1961. She was the Whitebrook Billeting Officer during the second world war. Photographer: Marie Hambrook, née Carstairs.

Folkestone and Birmingham evacuees who attended Whitebrook School, circa 1940. Folkestone teacher, Miss Woods, is standing at the back.
Front row - John Tiltman, Folkestone evacuee (1st on left), Anne Claxton, Folkestone evacuee (2nd from left), Donald Goddard, Birmingham evacuee (3rd from left), Mavis Bishop, Birmingham evacuee (4th from left), Sheila Tiltman, Folkestone evacuee (5th from left).
Second row back - Marie Carstairs (in checked dress), Folkestone evacuee (4th from right), Eileen Tompkinson, Folkestone evacuee (5th from right), Mary Marsh (curly hair), Folkestone evacuee (6th from right). Third row back - June Kemp, Folkestone evacuee (3rd from left).

The barn in the yard had double doors leading on to the road where the hay was unloaded and underneath were the calves, both sheds in the inner yard were for the milking cows and a small blacksmith's forge as that was Mr Higgins' trade.

Inside your back door there was a copper. Mrs Higgins used to make cheese. Off the kitchen there was a long passage used as a store and, in the second part, the barrels of cider (made at Tump Farm), then a room at the end with a big butter churn and a table with a trough in it to salt the bacon. On the left there was a room with a cheese press and animal food store. There was a door to the outside which I see has been filled in. I expect you still have the

daffodils in the field at the end of the garden as well as the lovely snowdrops. I used to pick and bunch them with a bit of evergreen and Mrs Higgins used to take them to Monmouth Market. I think I got 1/2d a bunch.

We used to have 'musical' Saturday evenings at The Bell. We children used to sit on the wall outside. Violet Morgan (The Tump) used to play the piano. We had many concerts and dances in the Village Hall. Joan Davies' mother, Maggie, was the pianist.

TAKEN FROM A LETTER DATED 8TH NOVEMBER 2001 FROM FORMER EVACUEE **MARIE HAMBROOK, NÉE CARSTAIRS, TO MR AND MRS GREGSON,** WHITEBROOK FARM.

Sisters, Violet (on the left) and Sheila Morgan, Tump Farm, circa 1940s.

1 Folkestone evacuees, October 1941. Left to right are, unknown boy, Eileen Tompkinson, Sheila Tiltman, John Tiltman and Valerie Tompkinson.

2 Two Folkestone families, the Tiltmans and the Tompkinsons, evacuated to The Old Post Office (now named 'Brook Cottage'), on the riverbank in Whitebrook, circa 1941.

3 The Old Post Office (now named 'Brook Cottage'), May 1941.

*Marie Carstairs
with her mother,
taken at the side of
the brook, circa
1948.
Marie was
evacuated from
Folkestone to
Clearwater Cottage
(The home of Mr
and Mrs Williams)
during the second
world war. Her
mother worked at
Glyncote Farm.*

JANUARY / FEBRUARY 1995

My mother got to know Bill Higgins in about 1951. My sister and I have no idea how she met him, it was probably a casual meeting while shopping in Newport, where my mother, sister and I lived. I spent time at the farm in 1952 onwards, when I was 12.

I remember a sense of shock when I met Bill for the first time. Mum and I were in the living room, the room to the right of the front door as you enter that way. He came up the steps from the kitchen which made even greater the impact of the fact that he was very short and round. He was perhaps 5' or maybe an inch or two more or less. He had white balding hair and he reminded me of Enid Blyton's Mr Pinkwhistle, a book I had had when younger.

Of course, Bill taught me to make butter. The churn was like a small shiny barrel on a stand. It was smooth inside and had brass fittings, with a sort of peep hole through which you could see the progress of the butter. It had a handle and you turned it continuously until you could hear the butter thudding down to the bottom as the churn revolved. This took forever and was very tiring. One day he caught me turning the handle with my foot, as my arms had got tired, and he called me all the lazy names under the sun. I couldn't see what the crime was – I'd got the same rhythm going and the butter came just the same! There was a big cheese press in the dairy too, also made of wood. Emily had used to make cheese but I don't think Bill did.

In retrospect my happiest times were the hours I spent collecting walnuts as they dropped from the two walnut trees above the house. I scoured the banks for them and day-dreamed all the while. I had an ongoing saga peopled with all sorts of characters – a mental soap opera and whilst I was doing that Bill was content and did not find other jobs for me to do. He was in fact well pleased as he had never had such a good haul of walnuts to sell. He stored them up in the front bedroom in the cupboard or dressing room off it, where the apples were stored. These also were for sale in Monmouth.

This has been rather a long account and I do hope that you have found it interesting. I have certainly enjoyed writing it. Reading through it I am aware that it is very much a child's eye view.

Visiting the farm certainly enriched my life.

TAKEN FROM A LETTER, DATED JAN / FEB 1995, FROM JENNIFER BALE, TO THE OWNERS OF WHITEBROOK FARM.

Marie Carstairs, Folkestone evacuee, at Glyncote Farm (now called 'Whitebrook Farm') with Rover (Bill Higgins' dog), circa 1940.

We first saw Whitebrook Farm, on the perfect day to nip in the bud all romantic dreams of living in the country. It was late November; bitterly cold. The wind was howling; the rain horizontal; a few ducks sulked under piles of dripping foliage.

We did the only sensible thing and made an offer on the spot. We have never regretted it.

Freud once said that in every marriage, four people, maybe six are in the bed (his parents, your parents, etc, etc) but in old houses like Whitebrook Farm, one is aware of a much bigger cast. What is now our bedroom was once where Bill Higgins laid his bald pink head. Marie Hambrook slept in the double bed with her mother when she was evacuated here during the war and before them came all the mill-owners; farmers; engineers; guest house keepers and lovers having illicit weekends. (We once found, behind a shed, a soggy old advertisement for the Whitebrook Farm Guesthouse. In it a dodgy looking couple were alighting from what looked like a Model T Ford.)

During our first week in Whitebrook, someone remarked doomily, that this place was "the graveyard of ambition." In some ways, it's true. Whitebrook, particularly in spring and summer, is the perfect place to bunk off, whether for a spot of riding, or wood chopping or what my father used to call "purposeful idling."

We've done all of this, but also enjoyed being able to work at home here and not spend frustrating hours driving, or queuing up, or stalled in traffic somewhere more purposeful. It's been the most fantastic bit of luck being able to live here.

JULIA GREGSON, WHITEBROOK FARM 2004.

JULIA GREGSON WAS BORN IN LONDON, BUT LIVED IN AMERICA AND AUSTRALIA, WHERE SHE WAS A JOURNALIST AND SHORT STORY WRITER BEFORE MOVING TO WALES. SHE IS WORKING ON HER SECOND NOVEL.

Whitebrook Farm, circa 1961. Photographer: Marie Hambrook, née Carstairs, former wartime evacuee at Clearwater Cottage.

Marie Carstairs, Folkestone evacuee, Bill Higgins (farmer and blacksmith at Glyncote Farm) and Rover, with the pigs at Glyncote Farm (now named 'Whitebrook Farm'), circa 1941.

Probably one of my strongest memories of growing up in Whitebrook, was my very first canter on my very first pony Simbre. I remember waking up and thinking to myself 'today I'm gonna do it!!' We set off with the essential witnesses, Mum, Dad and Dan (my best friend). As I reached the riverbank my stomach was full of butterflies, I was too nervous, Dan was going to HAVE to do it first. He did, very easily and I was furious at how brave he was, so with that I tugged him off, got a leg up onto Simbre and set off, first a gentle trot, then I gave one firm kick, and there it was, I finally cantered, a momentous day!

So many of my memories about Whitebrook are of the long summer evenings, playing in scented gardens, leaping over dustbins or hiding in trees and the disappointment when one of our parent's final shouts of 'supper' was heard. We knew the games were over and it was time to say goodnight. Once I was inside, caked in dirt, I was forced to have the dreaded bath. Luckily there was some entertainment with it as, if mum left the bathroom window open, I could watch the beloved ponies rolling and snorting in the field as the sun went in.

I loved going over to the Gaunt's house. The magical cupboard that Sarah stashed with biscuits and chocolates was always a selling point for me when Dan was trying to persuade me to come to his house. Admittedly to this day, I still make a beeline for that cupboard. When the infamous tree house was built at the Gaunts, I was a permanent resident. That was until the day I was trying to impress some of James' friends, by doing Tarzan inspired leaps from branch to branch, and unfortunately missed. I broke my arm. In a desperate attempt to help his hysterical friend, Dan told me to keep frantically moving my arm, probably one of the less treasured pieces of advice he has given me, but in the end, my arm was fine! I still love coming back to Whitebrook, it always has and always will be the place I think of as home. The longer I'm away from it the more I realise how beautiful it is and how lucky I was to grow up there.

POPPY GREGSON,
WHITEBROOK FARM 2004.

POPPY GREGSON WAS A PUPIL AT SEDDON HOUSE, TRELLECH SCHOOL AND FINALLY, STONAR SCHOOL IN WILTSHIRE. SHE IS NOW STUDYING PSYCHOLOGY, HISTORY AND ENGLISH AT NEWCASTLE UNIVERSITY. SHE HAS REPRESENTED GREAT BRITAIN IN THREE DRESSAGE TEAMS.

Watercolour of Glyncote Farm (now named 'Whitebrook Farm') by Brian Beale, Blackheath, Staffs, dated 24th June, 1943. He was on holiday at Glyncote to get away from the air raids. It was given to Folkestone evacuee Marie Carstairs and her mother.

Situated about 200 yards above The Glyn and formerly called Bridget's Mill, Wye Valley Mill, established in 1772 (Cross, undated), may have been built on an earlier wireworks. Power came from a small mill pond (now dry) and a stone dam extending along one side of the valley to form the leat. It is probable that paper was produced by hand as there is nothing in the remains, which are fairly substantial, pointing to steam power or the installation of machinery. This was one of the larger mills, which closed with the opening of the Wye Valley Railway. The mill-owner's house, Wye Valley House, still remains.

Main mill building and windows, taken from the south, Wye Valley Mill, circa 2004. Photographer: Adrian Gaunt.

Whitebrook is such a special place. The vast expanses of varied rural landscape meant that there were so many different avenues to explore. The water, the woodland, the huge pastures and so much wildlife are but a few of the aspects that characterise this little niche in the Wye Valley.

One of the pastimes I used to enjoy immensely was learning the art of rugby union in the garden. I remember being overwhelmed at the height and distance Dad could pass and kick the ball. I'm sure we used to play for hours on the bottom lawn and the nearest field, and I have no doubt that it was this grounding which helped to earmark my progression in this sport.

In my late teens I have particularly fond memories of the birthday parties that Mum and Dad have arranged for me. Kayaking down the River Wye followed by a hog roast and songs around the campfire is my ultimate idea of fun and relaxation. What a great way to celebrate your birthday.

I guess that gives one some idea of how special Whitebrook is to me. I find the area immensely relaxing. Whitebrook to me is one massive experience and I'm so lucky to know that I can develop and still be part of that whenever I venture home.

JAMES GAUNT, WYE VALLEY HOUSE, 23RD FEBRUARY 2004.

JAMES, A FORMER STUDENT OF MONMOUTH BOYS' SCHOOL, HAS PLAYED RUGBY FOR WALES UNDER 18 AND 19S AND ENGLAND STUDENTS. HE WENT TO EXETER UNIVERSITY AND, AT PRESENT, IS AT OXFORD. HE WAS AWARDED HIS OXFORD BLUE FOR RUGBY IN DECEMBER 2003.

Wye Valley House with mill ruins to the left (formerly the mill owner's house at Wye Valley Mills), circa 1985. Photographer: Adrian Gaunt.

I have lived next door to my best friend, Poppy, ever since day one. Pops and I were both lucky enough to have our own horses and from an early age we were granted the responsibility of going out riding on our own. If only our parents had known some of the crazy things we got up to then, that responsibility would soon have been banished! From the age of eight I have distinct memories of riding down to the river bank and putting our stirrups up as high as possible. What followed was a ferocious and highly personal race along the never-ending banks of the river Wye. We wouldn't stop for anything and many a time completely spoilt a poor fisherman's chance of ever catching a Wye Salmon (sorry Dad!). We too are probably the guiltiest victims of disturbing Tump Farm's cattle in breeding season as we stormed through the herd like hell for leather.

Another prominent memory of my younger years lies in the Wicked Whitebrook Bike Club. Every year after heavy rainfall myself, my big brother,

Pops, Dorothy and George would hop onto our BMX's and head for the huge puddles lying on the river bank behind the Everett's house. A couple of hours later we would return completely filthy and smelling like the backend of a baboon. It took us years to work out what lay in the bottom of those puddles…to this day I believe this was the Tump Farm cattle's way of repaying us for terrifying them as we tore along the river bank Lester Piggott style.

At the age of eleven I started at Monmouth Boys' School and it wasn't long before Whitebrook became the host of many school memories and tales. Before long Whitebrook Village Hall was the venue for the vast majority of our teenage discos. For many of us it was the first place where we experimented with alcohol, some were daring enough to have their first cigarette and, for the lucky amongst us, Whitebrook Village Hall holds the secrets of our first kiss!

On the subject of confessions I would also like to put my brother, James, into the

spotlight. I remember being woken up one morning and being told that today we were going to go 'menacing'! This involved various nasty little pranks but the one I particularly remember involved leaving a bucket full of dog dung on our unsuspecting neighbours' doorstep, to catch them out when they stepped out of the front door in slippers and dressing gown to collect their milk and morning newspapers. Anyone victim to the dog dung attack, please accept our apologies!

DAN GAUNT, WYE VALLEY HOUSE, 2004. DAN IS STUDYING AT NOTTINGHAM UNIVERSITY.

Dan Gaunt of Wye Valley House, circa early 1990s.

Main Picture - Opening of the village hall by Rt. Hon. Mr Forrestier-Walker, Conservative Candidate for Monmouth, circa 1926.

Village fete on the river bank circa, 1950. The villagers dressed as characters from 'The Archers'. Pictured from left to right are Colin Pick (Wye Mount), Daisy Morgan (Tump Farm), Donald Goddard (The Bell).

Village fete on the river bank, circa 1950. The villagers dressed up as characters from 'The Archers'.

Clearwater Mill, built in about 1760, was probably the first paper mill based in Whitebrook. It is situated some 600 yards upsteam from Wye Valley Mill (Cross, undated). The remains of an old mill pond further upstream, partial remains of a dam wall and a stone-lined leat running to the top of an old wheel pit probably relate to an earlier wire mill. A steam engine was installed in 1863, an overshot waterwheel and a 70 hp turbine (Coates, 1992). The capital expenditure does not appear to have paid off since the mill closed in 1875, having been made bankrupt.

A most interesting find of two note books was made by builders repairing a house near Clearwater Mill. They recorded timesheets and wages in 1859 / 60. In 1859 the total wages for six workmen were £3 12s 6d. per week. Women rag cutters were paid 9d. per cwt. and eight women shared a total of £1 3s 3d. (Gwent Record Office)

An iron pipe for carrying water from Manor Brook to drive the wheel at Clearwater Mill, circa 1990s. Photographer: Mike Sturt.

48

Clearwater Mill Ruins, circa 1990s.
Photographer: Mike Sturt.

Joy Wright on the railings in front of Manor Brook Cottage, circa 1940s. Joy and her two children, Susan and David, were evacuated to Clearwater House from Birmingham.

'Maybe I will start at the beginning as to how my husband and I were introduced to Clearwater House and the delightful village of Whitebrook. We loved the Wye Valley with its breath-taking scenery and at first stayed in a bungalow at Llandogo and then at Tintern. During one of our walks we saw a sign 'Clearwater Guest House' at the bottom of what we thought was a drive and therefore a private property, never realising it led to Whitebrook. A few years later we were recommended to Clearwater House - our first visit and the forerunner of so much happiness.

Boy Fowler (so called because he hated the name Aubrey) received compensation for a serious motorbike accident and with the money purchased Clearwater House; his mother-in-law and husband, Mr and Mrs Morgan, went into partnership and it was Mrs Morgan who made the guest house a success. She was a good cook and a real darling.

Actually, the first time we went, Greta wasn't married, she was a cashier in Woolworth's at Monmouth. I wish I had kept her wedding photo - she wore a blue crinoline dress - such a pretty girl, a true blonde with curls. Something that may interest you: At the time of taking possession of Clearwater House, Boy found various documents giving details of work and wages at the mill, as Clearwater was built by the owner. Boy gave these papers to a museum, but whether Monmouth or Chepstow he didn't state - could even have been Newport, but you could inquire if interested. The atmosphere at Clearwater was always a happy one. I imagined the owner's wife moving around in a crinoline. I wonder what happened to them and where they went. Enclosed is a snap I took of the mill chimney. Is it still there? When war was imminent the family insisted I went to Clearwater with the children and Mrs Morgan was happy to have us. She loved them and Susan had her first birthday there. Greta made a cake with one candle. My husband came at weekends when he could and brought either mother or father or my sisters. Clearwater was then bulging at the seams, as in addition, Mrs Morgan

sheltered 2 teachers and a mother with a small child. I had the room on the left with bedroom above. The little school was packed and I remember impetigo was rife and the teachers were scared of catching it. Whitebrook in those days buzzed with life. My little boy, David, loved to go to the halt to see the 4 o'clock go by, so most afternoons I took him and called at the PO on the way to purchase a bar of chocolate - it wasn't rationed then. I cannot imagine Whitebrook without the halt and trains going through. Sometimes I went with the children on the train to Monmouth to shop. It chugged along through the lovely tree covered hills - flame coloured in the Autumn. I was at Clearwater for $3^{1/2}$ months. As the bombing did not materialise I returned home to Birmingham - almost immediately into trouble. It is better not to dwell on those dark days. Over the years we continued to spend holidays at Clearwater. Eventually Mrs Morgan and husband left and took a cottage where Mr Morgan kept bees and sold honey. Greta couldn't really cope without her mother. We had one last holiday at

Clearwater before it was sold. Next visit was in a cottage by the brook with Greta and Boy. Greta then left and lived at the PO, so we stayed there. It seemed so strange passing by Clearwater and not entering the familiar door. Our last visit, we stayed at a little Inn. Greta had moved once again into a small cottage nearer to Tump Farm. Her father had died and her mother was very ill. My husband and I went to see her. As I left I felt very sad knowing I would not see her again. Little did I know then, that it would be my last visit to that lovely little valley, as a year or two later my husband died. He bought Haslingfield PO and lived there for 10 years. I had a bungalow built and have been a widow for 30 years.

This epistle has been a nostalgic trip into the past and I hope there will be something of interest in it, to you.

A TRANSCRIPTION OF A LETTER TO **MRS PORTER-DAVISON** (CLEARWATER HOUSE) FROM **MRS JOY WRIGHT**, WHO WAS EVACUATED FROM BIRMINGHAM WITH HER CHILDREN TO CLEARWATER HOUSE DURING 1939. IT WAS WRITTEN IN 1993 WHEN SHE WAS 86.

Aubrey 'Boy' Fowler (occupier of Clearwater House), his wife Greta and Mr Probert (landlord of The Bell) outside Clearwater House, circa 1940.

Harold Wright (husband of Joy Wright) and daughter Susan (aged 3) at Whitebrook Halt, circa 1941. Joy and her children were evacuated to Clearwater House, Whitebrook from Birmingham. Harold would travel to the village to visit them.

David Wright (aged 3), son of Joy Wright, outside Clearwater House, circa 1939. Joy Wright and her children were evacuated to Whitebrook from Birmingham.

Catapults – target practice took up a lot of our boyhood time. Miles and I would like to take this opportunity to apologise to the garden gnome community of Whitebrook – particularly the chap with the fishing rod who rashly chose a spot next to Mr. Townrow's pond, perilously close to the cover provided by the forest.

Milkman – 'Jack the Milk' also deserves an apology for the number of bangers set off under his van in the mornings, purely to hear the immortal exclamation "What the bloody hell was that!!!!".

BMX Bicycles – a lot of time was spent creating jumps on the track to recreate the best scenes from 'BMX Bandits'. These usually resulted in bruises, shouts for Mum and a lecture on the benefits of helmets, kneepads etc.

Wildlife – Miles seems to have had all the luck in this area, with otter and mink sightings near the stream and even one of the 'Big Cat' stalking the hedgerows. The most I ever saw was a dead fox, poisoned and curled as if sleeping behind a tree next to the track.

MARK PORTER-DAVISON,
10TH FEBRUARY 2004.
MARK AND HIS BROTHER MILES WERE BROUGHT UP AT CLEARWATER HOUSE, WHERE THEIR PARENTS STILL LIVE TODAY.

1 Mark and Miles Porter-Davison, outside their home, Clearwater House, 1988.

2 Group in doorway of Clearwater House, June 1940. Back row, left to right - Harry Morgan, Aubrey Fowler. Middle row, left to right - Mrs Morgan, Greta Fowler and Ida Tiltman. Front row, left to right - John Tiltman, Sheila Tiltman. The Tiltman family were evacuated to the Old Post Office (now named Brook Cottage) from Folkestone. Ida Tiltman and Gladys Tompkinson were sisters. Aubrey and Greta Fowler lived at Clearwater House. Mr and Mrs Morgan were Gretas parents.

Greta Fowler (occupied Clearwater House) with her mother, Annie Morgan, in doorway of Clearwater House, circa 1940s.

Sunnyside Mill was situated approximately one mile upstream from Clearwater Mill. Only the footings of the mill buildings remain and these now form part of the gardens of Traligael, the mill owner's house. Above the mill, on the opposite side of the valley, stands a chimney stack built in 1870. A long, stone-lined flue connected the chimney to the mill, presumably to carry the fumes away and provide draught. It was probably part of a modernisation scheme since by 1874 this mill had:-

- a 68 inch wide paper machine
- a 25 hp beam engine
- 2 horizontal steam engines of 15 and 5 hp
- 2 Cornish patent diagonal steam boilers
- 1 Wright's patent diagonal steam boiler
- Esparto boiling pans
- a 25 hp water turbine with a 50 ft fall of water.

THESE ITEMS WERE ADVERTISED FOR AUCTION ON THE CLOSURE OF THE MILL (COATES, 1992).

The chimney located 400ft from Sunnyside Mill, used for draught and to carry away the fumes from the mill, circa 1990s. Photographer: Mike Sturt.

Traligael, formerly the mill owner's house at Sunnyside Mill, circa 1960s.
© The Nelson Museum, Monmouth.

EDWARD AND MARION LYSAGHT

Edward Lysaght was born in 1898 to a wealthy manufacturer who set up the Orb steelworks in Newport. Edward worked in the family firm and ran it after his father's death until 1952.
He then became Deputy Chairman of Guest, Keen and Nettlefold.

He married Marion who was described as the most beautiful woman in Gwent. Initially they lived at The Conagar and then moved in 1970 to Traligael where they opened their garden to the public in aid of charities.

Edward served in the Home Guard and subsequent owners of Traligael were shocked when their builders threw an old box on a bonfire, only to have it explode as it contained his wartime bullets! In 1953 he became High Sheriff of Monmouth.

Not only did he make a financial contribution towards the building of the Village Hall and made bequests to the

church, Edward also bought land adjoining Cleddon Bog to save it from harm. He was certainly ahead of his time in conservation matters.

He was a landscape painter and exhibited his works in various British galleries (including in London), the National Library of Wales and in Australia.

Edward Lysaght as a baby, circa 1900. He spent his later years at Traligael.

Tal-y-Bont Hunt Ball, 1931. Edward Lysaght (later of Traligael) is seated at centre front. Marion (his wife) is the first lady on the left at the back.

Fernside Mill is perhaps the most impressive because, from the exterior, it is intact and adds character to the mill owner's house, standing beside a mill pond. The mill is a three storey building. The two lower floors housed the plant and machinery, the top floor being used as a drying area of open slatted construction. Below the mill is a stable block for ten horses. In 1816 there were four mills in existence. On the assumption that the highest mill upstream was last to be built, Fernside may not have been built until after 1816 (Tucker, 1971). The first reference to Fernside Mill appears in 1868 when the owners were Green & Co. who owned the mill until 1875.

Nothing on the site points to the installation of steam engines and it may mean that unlike other mills in the valley, it was never modernised. Some water tanks are situated near the mill and are believed to relate to a trout rearing concern in the 1920s.

"A charming story is related by Mr Pick who heard from his mother who saw the lovely Fernside Mill, full of women and girls, each armed with a pair of large, cutting scissors, all singing as they worked at cutting up the rags into smaller pieces." (Harris, 1968)

Letter dated 27th June 1884, from W. Wilson of Fernside Mills to Mr James.

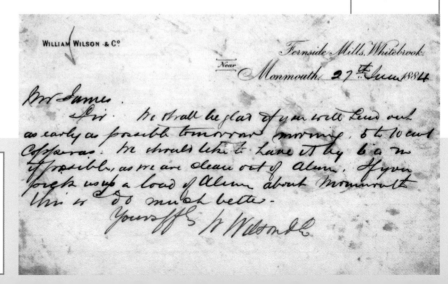

Pen and ink of Fernside Mill House by Debbie Devauden (formerly of Maes Llymysten, Whitebrook).

Fernside Mill House

ELVER FISHING IN WHITEBROOK

For three months of the year elver fishing still goes on in Whitebrook but local people are no longer involved. Prior to the 1980s many inhabitants used to supplement their larder and their purses by spending nights on the river banks waiting for the elvers to arrive. They used lamps to attract the creatures nearer to the bank and then wielded special nets made of hazel and muslin. The shape is strange, looking like a baby's crib on a handle. The frames were manufactured at a saw mill on the bank opposite Llandogo and steamed to make the wood bend. They were hung on apple trees to dry. A net made in this way would last a man a lifetime. Modern nets are made of metal and synthetic fabric and are much heavier. Last autumn a BBC 4 programme 'Moving On' featured Roger Brown, who owns the shop in Llandogo, talking about his recollections of elver fishing. His grandfather, who had captained one of the river boats until this occupation ended with the building of the railway line, then organised the family to help him harvest the eels. Subsequently Roger's father became a successful elverer and drafted Roger at the age of seven into the team. His task initially was to hold the lamp and he was often in trouble for doing things wrong but he gradually acquired the necessary skills.

In those days catches were large so, although the elvers were relatively cheap, the activity made a big difference to the local economy. It was hard work both by day and night. Once caught, the elvers had to be cleaned and then put in a large boiler full of cold water which was gently brought to the boil. Joan Davies who has always lived in Whitebrook remembers helping to clean the elvers and then watching them being poured into the big copper at Tump Farm. According to Roger, his mother used to drain the boiled catch and put it in a press to make elver cheese. Since there was no refrigeration elvers had to be sold the same day, either from local shops or by taking them round to the local pubs that evening.

Roger's favourite spot was by Bigsweir Bridge. Women as well as men took part in catching the fish and it was a friendly activity with people from Llandogo, Whitebrook, Brockweir and St Briavels all participating. Now elvers are so expensive and there are so few of them that it is highly competitive. In his broadcast Roger described what he called his coming of age. One night when he was fifteen he started fishing on his own until so many elvers appeared that he had to accept help from an older man called Billy Evans who used to work in the tin works at Redbrook. They spent most of the night collecting their harvest and filled every container they had. Roger had to go home in the morning to fetch his father's tractor to transport the catch back home.

Roger no longer has time to fish but plans to resume his activities when he retires. He still makes elver cheese for special occasions but only a handful of local people, other than his family, eat elvers any more. They now cost £140 a kilo and since they shrink to half the weight when cooked they are as much a luxury as caviare or truffles.

Wye Valley Fisheries Lorry, circa mid 1920s. The Wye Valley Fisheries, Whitebrook was situated on the site of Fernside Mill.

During the 1830s a decision was taken to build the Holy Trinity Chapel of Ease with an attached school-room. Among the list of subscribers was Captain Rooke of Bigsweir House, who gave the site for the church. In addition, many of the craftsmen and labourers employed to build the Holy Trinity contributed cash as well as their skills.

The church, excluding the school-room, was 44 feet long and 29 feet wide with a porch on its west end. The school-rooms, of which there were two, were built on the south east wall of the church, the hill being cut back to make space for them. The school received no sun and there was always a problem with damp.

During the 1930s the school, which could accommodate approximately 30 pupils, was put on the education authority's list of schools with defective premises and repairs were carried out in the late 1930s. Thereafter the school accommodated infants and juniors only, older children travelling daily to Monmouth.

THE SCHOOL CLOSED DURING THE 1950s AND THE CHURCH IN 2004.

View of The Bell and the Holy Trinity Church.

1 Holy Trinity Church, January 1987.

2 Paintings for Reredos by Mrs H E Sheppard and Miss Digby of Newland, displayed in screens at Holy Trinity Church.

Whitebrook School Fancy Dress, circa 1930. Colin Pick (back row, left), Reg Hussey (back row, centre), Phyllis Fowler (front row, centre), Florence Price (front row, right).

Whitebrook School, circa early 1940s, includes local children and evacuees. Whitebrook teacher, Miss Butcher is on the left at the back. Birmingam teacher Megan Jones (arrived with Birmingham evacuees) is 2nd from the right, at the back. Folkestone Teacher, Miss Woods (arrived with Folkestone evacuees) is on the right, at the back.

1 Whitebrook School, circa 1890s. Grace Amelia Ida Crum
(wearing spectacles), Nell Crum (3rd on her left).

2 Whitebrook Council School, circa 1920s.

The Pick family at Pool House, Penallt, including William (1845-1916) and Eliza (1847-1922) Pick, middle row, 3rd and 4th from left, circa 1912. The Pick family attended Whitebrook Baptist Chapel and William Pick owned a barge, which he used for Baptist Chapel outings down the Wye.

The Baptist Chapel was built in 1829 and enlarged in 1831. A day school and Sunday School were opened in 1853 and a new schoolroom was built in 1855.

The chapel closed in 1989 and is now being converted into a private dwelling.

The graveyard contains some interesting headstones of former Whitebrook papermakers Edward Johnson who died in 1845 and William Ede who died in 1891. In addition, many members of the Pick family, a prominent family within the Whitebrook Valley, are buried there.

1 Colin Pick and his wife Dorothy, pictured with Colin's mother Gwen, Wye Mount, circa 1940. The Pick family ran the Post Office. Colin was in the airforce.

2 Francis William Pick, proprietor of Whitebrook PO in the 1920s, 30/10/1890 – 30/04/1959), First World War photograph.

Whitebrook Baptist Chapel, circa 1990s.
Photographer: Mike Sturt.

GO TO
FRANCIS W. PICK,
POST OFFICE STORES,
-:- WHITEBROOK, -:-
For the
Best Value in BREAD (homebaked),
GROCERIES and PROVISIONS.

Your Patronage Respectfully Solicited.

1 Gwen and Francis Pick, Wye Mount, circa 1940s. They were the proprietors of the Post Office.

2 Gwendolyn May Pick, née Golder (04/05/1895 – 03/11-1983) and Francis William Pick (30/10/1890 – 30/04/1959), proprietors of Whitebrook PO, circa late 1920s.

3 Advert in Llandogo and Whitebrook Monthly Magazine, February 1922.

MAVIS PEARSALL (NÉE BISHOP) first set foot in the Wye Valley in 1939. She had been evacuated to Roseleigh, the home of Harold & Edith Wilkins in Penyfan, from her school in Camden Street, Birmingham. Mavis, aged 5, and her sister, Kathleen, aged 7, attended Whitebrook school during their first winter here and made many excursions to the village before they returned home in 1945.

One of her recollections involves picking snowdrops and wild daffodils near to her temporary home, parcelling them up in a shoe box and sending them to her mother in Birmingham. Her mum was so thrilled that she would distribute them amongst her friends. Mavis would also collect snowdrops with Mrs Wilkins. These were bunched and sold on a stall at Monmouth market. The beauty and profusion of wild daffodils and snowdrops has stuck in her mind after all these years.

Mavis recalls the time she and her sister trudged up the lane past the Baptist Chapel, which they sometimes attended, on a cold and bitter winter's day. The road was very slippery and they couldn't get their footing. She remembers bursting into tears when a lady from one of the houses came out and wrapped rags around their shoes, providing enough grip so that they could get home to Penyfan.

Birmingham evacuees pictured outside the Holy Trinity Church with Birmingham teacher (Megan Jones), circa 1940.
Pictured are Donald Goddard, The Bell (far left), Mavis Bishop (3rd girl from left) and Kathleen Bishop (last girl on right). Sisters, Mavis and Kathleen were evacuated to Roseleigh, Penyfan, the home of Harold and Edith Wilkins.

THE DARKNESS OF SUNNYBANK
By JON GOLDING

The last thing on our minds when we moved from the city to our new home, an extended old cottage, was the darkness of the countryside night. The dark had never worried either of us before, still doesn't now, although it plays a larger part in our lives than we could have imagined. The orange halo of eternal twilight that we took for granted in the city was gone. Torches replaced mobile phones as essential items; outside lights were fitted on every corner of the building, left on through daylight if we knew we were returning late.

We moved in the depth of winter when the inky blackness was at its most oppressive, seemingly thick enough to inhale on nights when the moon was waning or the cloud cover too thick. Even during the summer, when the night-time is relatively short, it feels almost comforting to wake to what you could imagine a world of blindness to be like and raise an invisible hand within an inch of your face. At first, the darkness seemed reassuring, like an extra blanket on a cold night, holding you in its embrace. As long as the alarm wasn't squawking on the bedside table, it was easy to return to comfortable sleep. After all, what's there to be scared of about darkness? It's not the dark that scares us but what our minds tell us it's hiding or what we fear will reveal itself from within. After all, we are flight animals; our bodies are apparently engineered to react to what frightens us. Return home to a dark house on a winter's night when there are no lights left on and we can imagine anything, our minds will heighten our anxieties as it prepares us to react quickly should the need arise. Sleep nullifies this. Our senses, like our bodies, are relaxed, our imagination somewhere more pleasing. Even as we wake, the dregs of our dreams slip through our minds like sand between our fingers. What was clear one minute is gone the next. Our guards are down; we are at our most vulnerable.

Somewhere in the no man's land between dreams and wakefulness, it rushed at me. I knew then and I know now, I was awake. The dream I awoke from was a calm one, something about old friends reliving an experience. Whatever came at me, it wasn't born from the residue of unhappy times revisited. It was no flick from a demon's tail, trying to draw me back into a nightmare. I know what I saw, and it scared the hell out of me.

I remember waking, registering how dark the night seemed and sitting up to fluff my pillow. Sarah, my wife, was sound asleep. I was about to rejoin her. I can't remember it making a sound as it leapt out of the darkness. Something was thrown towards me. I cried out, through surprise rather than fear and leapt from the bed. Light exploded around me and I felt the cold wooden floor on my skin as I tried to crawl under the bed, my arms working furiously to disentangle myself from whatever it was that I'd seen rushing at me. I felt very frightened. Sarah collapsed into a giggling heap, sure that I had simply fallen out of bed. I explained to her that something had rushed at me out of the darkness,

Sunnybank, circa 2003.

throwing some sort of net over me. I figured that it was weighted, as it unfurled like a spiders web as it came towards me. I was attempting to get the net off me as I scrambled under the bed. It sounded reasonable to me, but Sarah once again collapsed in hysterics.

We still laugh about it now and Sarah tells the story well. I love to watch the expressions change on peoples' faces as she recounts it, especially the last part. Sarah added that later after she'd told the story in the local pub. As usual, the part about the net being thrown over me always raised the loudest laugh. At first, she always told it in a guess-what-he-fell-out-of-bed-and-thought-he'd-been-attacked-by-a-ghost sort of way. On this occasion, a man we hardly knew asked us where we lived. Someone answered for us, as Sunnybank was well known to the locals. Many of the previous owners had used the pub themselves. They knew one of them particularly well, he was a bit of a local character and had lived and died alone at the cottage. He was a local poacher, someone who made his way in the world selling stolen salmon for a

good price in the days before supermarkets made farmed salmon cheaper than chips. Calmly, the chap explained to us the local practice for catching fish in the fast flowing brooks along the Wye Valley. After that, the story and particularly the ending, took a more sinister meaning to us. According to everyone that night, and many others since, the usual method of catching fish is to throw a weighted net over them as they lie still in a quiet brook. Apparently, the technique was best employed on dark nights when the fish rest in pools as if asleep.

The strangest fact of all became clear after we researched historic census information. The oldest part of the house, the part where our bedroom is located, dates back to the 17th century. According to the records, many of the male residents over this period are listed as fishermen. Most, if not all, were probably poachers.

JON GOLDING, THE SON OF A COAL MINER FROM THE CYNON VALLEY, WAS BORN IN ABERGAVENNY IN 1965. EDUCATED IN BRECON AND UNIVERSITY COLLEGE, LONDON, HE CURRENTLY WORKS FOR COCA COLA IN LONDON.

JON HAS WRITTEN SEVERAL ARTICLES AND MANY SHORT STORIES, SOME OF WHICH HE HOPES TO HAVE PUBLISHED IN THE COMING YEAR.

FOLLOWING FOUR WONDERFUL YEARS IN WHITEBROOK, JON AND HIS WIFE SARAH RECENTY MOVED TO DORSET WITH THEIR YOUNG SON JOSHUA.

A FINAL NOTE

In 2003 Whitebrook Conservation Group decided to increase the scope of its work from conservation 'on the ground' to include the preservation of photographs and historical records. There was a recognition that, as each year passed, more and more sources might be lost. After appealing for photographs and other records, it staged the *Then & Now* Exhibition in March 2004. It was clear from the reactions of visitors to the exhibition that permanent records should be produced. This publication is one of these. A fuller version of the Whitebrook *Then & Now* Archive will be available on DVD.

Then & Now is, in part, an attempt to track some of the social and economic changes in this small South Wales community over roughly two centuries. The archive displays changes in industry (the rise and demise of the mills), communications (the arrival and closure of Whitebrook Halt) and people's dwindling dependency on the land and natural environment as a means of survival as well as a source of income.

In the main, the archive comprises a photographic record of these changes accompanied by written accounts. Some of the written recollections are taken from letters whilst others were written and collected specifically for the *Then & Now* project. Readers of this publication and users of the DVDs can decide for themselves whether lifestyles in the Whitebrook Valley are better today than in the past.

Sadly there are gaps in the history of the archive as pictures and documents do not remain depicting all aspects of Whitebrook village life. If any additional information comes to light, we would encourage its owners to contact Whitebrook Conservation Group or The Nelson Museum, Monmouth so that it is preserved for posterity.

It is hoped that this project will be used by a broad spectrum of people – school children, students, local families, genealogists, historians, businesses, former, present & future residents of the community and anyone who is interested.

We should like to think that it will encourage people to recognise the importance of preserving both the built and natural environment of the Whitebrook area and to see scope for this in other communities. In this connection, readers are most welcome to contact Whitebrook Conservation Group for advice on setting up similar projects.

Whilst this archive has been very much a community effort, we should like to thank Steve Dale for his artistic flair and enthusiasm. We should also like to thank Rob Golder for his patience and for lending his technological experience so willingly towards the creation of the DVDs.

**ELEANOR REES & DIANA BEVAN
WHITEBROOK CONSERVATION GROUP.**

Bibliography

Coates, S. D., *The Water Powered Industries of the Lower Wye Valley, The River Wye from Tintern to Redbrook* (Monmouth: Monmouth Borough Museums Service, 1992).

Cross, A. G. R., *Old Industrial Sites in Wyedean – A Gazetteer* (undated & no publisher).

Harris, P. G., *Wye Valley Industrial History*, (1968).

Lease dated 6th June 1607 between the Earl of Pembroke & Montgomery and Governors Assistants and the Society of the City of London for the Mineral and Battery Works, Gwent Record Office, 4806, M446.

Tucker, D. G., 'The Embanked Ponds of the Penallt – Whitebrook – Redbrook Area and Their Industrial Uses', *Severn and Wye Review*, Vol. 1, No. 3 Spring, 1971.

Tucker, D. G., 'The Paper Mills of Whitebrook, Monmouthshire', *Archaeologia Cambrensis*, (1972).

Tucker, D. G., 'The beginning of the wireworks at Whitebrook, Gwent in the early seventeenth century'. From a collection of notes belonging to the late Prof. Tucker at Monmouth Museum.

Williams-Davies, J., 'The Travelling Cidermaker', *Folk Life*, Vol. 29 (1990 – 1991).

1841 Census (Llandogo), HO107 / 747. Copy available at Gwent Record Office.
1851 Census (Llandogo), HO107 / 2445. Copy available at Gwent Record Office.

Acknowledgments

Whitebrook Conservation Group is grateful to the following for funding, without which we could not have produced a permanent record.

Monmouthshire County Council

Rural Community Action Monmouthshire

Trellech Community Council (for both financial assistance and the use of their laptop and scanner)

Welsh Assembly Government

Wye Valley Area of Outstanding Natural Beauty Office

Whitebrook Conservation Group would like to thank the following for permission to include copyright material and also, in some instances, for help and advice given. In some cases it has not been possible to trace the owners of photographs, but Whitebrook Conservation Group would be pleased to hear from any further copyright owners of material used in this book.

Jennifer Bale
Susan Beustead
Jo & Ken Binmore
Lena Bishop
Maggie Biss
Rosie Biss
Roger Brown
Joan Davies
Debbie Devauden
Austin Durrant
Derwena Evans
David Foster
Adrian & Sarah Gaunt
Dan Gaunt
James Gaunt
Vicki Gaunt
Rob Golder
Jonathon Golding
Julia Gregson
Poppy Gregson
Marie Hambrook
Mrs V. E. Heales
Mrs F. C. Hussey
Keith Lewis & family
Mary Lewis
Helen Marshall
Ross Morgan
Mavis Pearsall
Clarice Porter
Mark Porter-Davison
Sue Porter-Davison
John Prince
Terry Price
Lord Raglan

Allen & Nerys Rees
Mrs Reynolds
Anne Tiggy Roberts
Martin Routh
Barbara Sobey
Mike Sturt
Hazel & Peter Symes
Glynis Taylor
Ashley Thomas
Mike Tiltman
Doreen Warmington-Gardner
Mary Whitmore
Austyn Williams

Staff at
Forest & Wye Valley Review
The Forester
The Monmouthshire Beacon
The Monmouth Free Press
The Western Daily Press

The Nelson Museum, Monmouth – Andrew Helme, Sue Miles and Dan Groucott.

We have received so many offers of help and so much information where, in some instances, we have not been advised of the names of the donors. Please accept our apologies if we have omitted your name(s).

Finally this book, due to space constraints, cannot encompass the whole of the information made available to us. We are nevertheless most grateful to those who have contributed in any way.